junior dramascripts

Cinderella

Adapted by
Guy Williams

with production notes by
Ginny Lapage

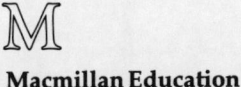

Macmillan Education

FOREWORD

JUNIOR DRAMASCRIPTS aim:
- to provide enjoyment
- to extend language development through individual or group reading
- to offer material for performance.

In the development of language, play-reading provides a valuable cooperative activity. The members of a mixed-ability group reading together with or without supervision will tend to support each other. They may have the discipline of knowing that a task is to be completed after the reading is over. This task may involve discussion of the play; the performance of part or all of the play to the class; or the mounting of a display in the classroom or elsewhere.

If performance is intended, improvisation around the theme, events and characters in the scripts being studied is considered most useful if it takes place before the members of a class are given their scripts. This ensures that the children's interpretations are more natural and that, in consequence, they find it easier to speak and learn their lines. Improvisation also helps children to understand the characters in a play and to explore ways of interpreting their ideas. The children involved become increasingly self-confident as they are absorbed in the theme of the play.

The production and performance of a JUNIOR DRAMASCRIPT can teach a great deal, since this will require careful planning and will call for teamwork and cooperation. A great deal will depend on the age and ability of the group and the aims of the teacher. If a child prefers not to act, then he or she will have the choice of many other equally rewarding tasks. Research may have to be carried out before the scenery, costumes and properties are designed. Plans for the set, sound and lighting may be made as part of art, craft, science and maths lessons. And, every member of a production team will have an important part to play:

The Stage Manager will have to make sure that everyone and everything is in the right place, and at the right time.

The Lighting Technician will have to make sure that the right lighting effects are correctly timed to coincide with the action.

The Sound Technician will have to think of, and provide, live or recorded sound effects. This may be done in a music lesson with, possibly, the help of a class.

The members of a *Publicity Team* will have to think of ways of publicising the performances with posters, or by other means.

The Front of House Manager will have to count the seats, sell or allocate tickets, and organise stewards or ushers for each performance.

Younger children will enjoy helping teachers, or older companions,by contributing ideas. Parents and other interested parties may be involved in the provision of scenery, costumes and properties, or by being asked to help in other ways. All, if given clear directives and encouraged to aim for excellence, will gain much satisfaction from this cooperative activity. And, the performances themselves will provide much pleasure for the families and friends who support the school.

GUY WILLIAMS
Advisory Editor

THE PEOPLE IN THE PLAY

CINDERELLA (or 'CINDERS', for short). She is the daughter of a Baron, and she is bullied by the Baron's new wife and the new wife's two ugly daughters

BUTTONS, the Baron's manservant, who tries to protect Cinders

THE BARON, who lives in a Castle

THE BARON'S SECOND WIFE

AMANDA
BELINDA } the Ugly Sisters

THE POSTMAN, who brings letters to the Castle

CINDERELLA'S FAIRY GODMOTHER, who can do wonderful things by magic

A COACHMAN

SIX GROOMS, to walk behind the Coachman's coach

THE KING

THE QUEEN

THE PRINCE, their son, and heir to the throne

FOOTMEN, and OTHER SERVANTS at the Palace

GUESTS AT THE BALL

THE PLAY

Scene One

(*A Kitchen in a Castle.* **Cinders** *enters. She is dirty, and wearing rags. She hides in a corner, by the hearth. Then* **Buttons** *comes in, to start the story.*)

Buttons　In this Castle, with his wife,
A bumbly Baron spends his life . . .

(**The Baron** *comes into view. Then* **Buttons** *says*)

. . . He had a loving wife before.
She is dead. She is no more.
His second wife would be no loss.
She is FIERCE and she is CROSS.

(**The Baron's Wife** *can be heard calling, from the distance* 'HUSBAND! HUSBAND! WHERE ARE YOU?')

The Baron (*Calling back*)　Here, my little Tweeky-Boo!

Buttons　She has two bossy daughters, too.
A plainer pair you never met.

(**Amanda** *and* **Belinda** *enter. They are ugly but they are dressed in new, clean clothes.*)

Amanda (*To* **The Baron**)　Hello, Poppa!

The Baron　Hello, Pet!

Belinda　Where's that awful Cinders? . . .

(*She calls*)

. . . Quick,
Cinders! . . .

(*Seeing* **Cinders** *in her corner, she aims a kick at her half-sister and shouts*)

1

. . . Oh, you make me sick!
Get up! You lazy beggar, you!
Or I'll beat you black and blue!

The Baron   Belinda, dear, I am her Dad!

Belinda   I don't care. She makes me mad!

(**The Baron's Wife** *flounces in.*)

The Baron's Wife   She makes you cross? I quite agree.
Is any girl as slow as she?
She'd better wake up. . . .

(*To* **Cinders,** *she says*)

. . . Understand?
Don't ask me to lend a hand.

The Baron (*To* **His Wife**)
Dearest! Now you are my wife
You must have an easy life.
No more washing-up for you –
Cooking's over. Sweeping, too.

The Baron's Wife (*Looking fondly at* **Her Daughters**)
And my girls are not allowed
To do the house-work. They're too proud.

Amanda   House-work? What a mad idea!
Cinders does it. That's quite clear!

Belinda   Go on, Cinders. Get a broom.
Tidy up, and sweep the room.

The Baron's Wife   Wash the dishes. Clean the stairs.
Dust the tables! And the chairs!

Amanda   Get the work done, while we play . . .

(*To* **Belinda,** *she says*)

. . . Come on, Sister. Let's away!

(**Amanda** *and* **Belinda** *go out.*)

The Baron's Wife (*To* **The Baron**)
>Come, my husband. We'll go, too.
>We've some adding-up to do.
>Let's count our cash! Let's have a laugh!. . . .

>(*She chuckles, and then says*)

>. . . With Cinders here, we save on Staff!

(The Baron *and* **His Wife** *go out*)

Cinders (*Beginning to sweep*)
>Dust and cobwebs; dirt and fluff –
>Don't I sweep these floors enough?
>Sweeping near and sweeping far,
>The more I sweep, the worse they are.

Buttons   Let me help you, Cinders dear.
>You'll be worn out soon, I fear.

Cinders   I'll brush and scrub until I tire
>Then I'll sit down by the fire,
>In the cinders, in the dirt . . .

>(*She sits down suddenly and says*)

>. . . Oh, my poor legs! How they hurt!

(Amanda *comes back and sees* **Cinders** *sitting down.*)

Amanda (*Crossly*)   Come, you idle creature! Who
>Told you that a rest was due?
>You must work until you drop.
>We will whip you if you stop.

(Amanda *makes sure that* **Cinders** *is hard at work again before she goes out.*)

Cinders (*To* **Buttons**, *as she sweeps*)
>Mother was so sweet and kind:
>The dearest person one could find.
>I was sad, the day she died.

3

Buttons Then your Dad brought home this bride.
Where he found her, Heaven knows!
In some jumble, I suppose.
He really made a bad choice there.
And her daughters! What a pair!

Cinders They're not too bad. They might be worse.

Buttons They would make an angel curse.
You're too gentle, Cinders, dear.
You let them bully you, I fear.

Cinders Oh, well, yes. Perhaps I do.
But nobody is bad all through.

Buttons Poor old Cinders! . . .

(*He takes her broom, saying*)

. . . Give it me!
I'm good at sweeping. Just you see!

(*There is a knock at the door.*)

Cinders Someone knocking at our door!

Buttons The Postman's knock! He's been before!

(**Cinders** *goes to the door.*)

The Postman Something wonderful, I bring.
Here's a letter from the King.

Cinders From the King?

The Postman It's not for you.
It is for the other two.

(**Amanda** *rushes into the Kitchen.*)

Amanda Cinders! What have you got there?
Hand it over! . . .

(**Belinda** *rushes into the Kitchen.*)

Belinda (*To* **Cinders**) Just you dare

4

Touch it with your dirty hands!

Amanda (*Reading the front of the letter*)
'POSTED BY THE KING'S COMMANDS.'

Belinda   One foot long. Six inches wide.
Break the seal, Sis. What's inside?

Amanda (*Reading the letter from* **The King**)
'My son the Prince is now a man.
He'll find a wife. I'm sure he can.
So, to help him with his quest,
Come to our Ball. Please wear your best.'

Belinda   A Ball! A Ball! Oh, what a joy!
The Prince is such a handsome boy!

Amanda (*Calling loudly*)   Poppa! Poppa! . . .

(**The Baron** *comes into the Kitchen and* **Amanda** *says*)

         . . . Listen here!
We're going to a Ball, Old Dear.
We've had a letter from the King.
Isn't that a splendid thing?

The Baron   A Ball? How nice! A royal 'do'?
What an honour for you two!
Now, we'd better tell your Mum! . . .

(*He calls*)

         . . . Wifey! Tweeky! Come! Come! Come!
Leave the cash! We've got some news!

Belinda   Shall I wear my Size Ten Shoes?

The Baron   While you wonder what to wear
I'll find a coach, to get you there.
There's sure to be one, in the yard.
We've not sold all, though times are hard.

(**The Baron** *hurries away*)

Amanda   Cinders! Fetch my finest gown!

5

(**Cinders** *also hurries away.*)

Belinda　Buttons! Bring our jewels down!

(**Buttons**, *too, skips off*)

Amanda (*Calling*)　Mother! Come and give a hand! . . .

(*She says to* **Belinda**)

. . . At the Ball, we must look grand!

Belinda　All the Lords and Ladies there
Will be dressed with special care . . .

(*As* **The Baron's Wife** *comes into the Kitchen,* **Belinda**
says)

. . . We're going to the Palace, Ma!
For a Ball. Not you! Not Pa!

Amanda　It's US. It's not an Old Folks' Dance.
It's for the young. You've had your chance!

(**Cinders** *brings a party gown.*)

Belinda (*to* **Amanda**)　You can't wear that. You're much too big!

Amanda (*To* **Cinders**)　Cinders! Go and get my wig!

Belinda　Cinders! Go and get my pearls!
And bring a dozen pin-on curls! . . .

(*As* **Cinders** *goes out again,* **Belinda** *calls*)

. . . BUTTONS! . . .

(*When* **Buttons** *comes with a box of jewels, she says*)

. . . Go and get my fan!
Hurry up, you lazy man! . . .

(*As* **Buttons** *goes out again, she says*)

. . . Why we keep him, I don't know.

Amanda　We'll get Pop to let him go . . .

6

(*She calls*)

... Cinders! Cinders! Where's that girl?

Belinda   I'd like to wear this pretty pearl.
I fear my neck's a little ...

Amanda   ... Fat?

Belinda   No, I'd hardly call it that.
Say – It's on the solid side.

Amanda (*Calling again*)   Cinders! Here! I'll flay your hide!

(**Cinders** *comes back into the Kitchen with* **Amanda's** *wig.*)

Belinda (*To* **Cinders**)   Do my hair, you stupid lump!
When I call you, jump! Jump! Jump!

(*With* **The Baron's Wife** *and* **Cinders** *helping,* **Amanda** *and* **Belinda** *dress themselves up.*)

Amanda   Now! The glass! ...

(**Cinders** *brings a mirror and* **Amanda**, *pleased with herself, says*)

... I look a treat!

The Baron's Wife   Yes, my dear. You both look sweet!

(**Buttons** *comes back with a fan.*)

Buttons (*To* **Belinda**)   Here you are, Miss! Here's your fan!

Belinda   That's my mother's. Stupid man!

(*She throws it at him as* **The Baron** *comes back into the Kitchen.*)

The Baron   The coach is waiting, now, outside
Are you ready for your ride?

Amanda   Yes, we are. Come, watch us mount ...

(*To* **Cinders**)

. . . I don't mean you. You do not count.

Belinda   She must not be allowed to slack!

Amanda (*To* **Cinders**, *again*)
Mind you work till we get back!

(**Amanda** *and* **Belinda** *sweep out, followed by* **The Baron** *and* **His Wife**, *and* **Buttons**.)

Cinders (*To* **Herself**)   If I had a hundred wishes,
I would dump all dirty dishes.
I would simply throw away
The pots and pans I scour each day . . .

(**Her Fairy Godmother** *enters the Kitchen, and* **Cinderella** *says*)

. . . A visitor? What brings you here?

The Godmother   I'm your Godmother, my dear.
When I wave my magic wand
All the world I can command.
And now, my darling. Left behind?
Not invited? That's unkind!
Do not worry. I am here.
I'll get you to the Ball, my dear.

Cinders   Oh, how gladly I'd go there!
But I have no clothes to wear.

The Godmother   Clothes and coach and jewels, too,
Will come by fairy grace to you.
First – into the garden go.
Find the pumpkins, in a row.
Pick the biggest of them all.
That will take you to the Ball.

Cinders   But how . . .?

The Godmother   Leave things to me.
You, a fairy coach will see.
And, six horses would be nice.

Tell me, have we any mice?

Cinders   In the trap.

The Godmother   Then set them free,
And six horses they will be.
One fat coachman we must find,
And six grooms to walk behind.
A rat, I think, will do the trick.
And six lizards. Find them, quick! . . .

(**Cinders,** *excited, runs out and* **The Godmother** *says*)

. . . Cinders does deserve a treat.
She's ill-used, and still she's sweet.
Now, I'll get her to the Ball.
That's the greatest treat of all!

(*She waves her wand, and* **A Coachman** *comes into the Kitchen. He bows to* **The Godmother.**)

The Coachman   Yesterday, I was a rat
Making faces at the cat.
Now, that's past, I know not how.
I'm driving six grey horses now.

(*Another wave of the wand, and* **Six Grooms** *enter the Kitchen. They bow to* **The Godmother.**)

The First Groom   An hour ago, I was a lizard.
Now I'm not. I think a wizard
Has been playing funny tricks.
I'm a servant. One of six.

(**The First Groom** *shows* **The Other Five** *how to be good attendants.*)

The Godmother   Now, I'll get my darling dressed.
She must be the grandest guest.
She shall have a gorgeous gown,
The finest cloak in any town.
All her shyness she will lose

When I give her two glass shoes.
No one dancing will compare
With my Cinders. That I swear! ...

(*She waves her wand again, and* **Cinders** *comes in,
dressed for the Ball.* **All** *clap and bow.* **The Godmother**
gazes at her and says)
... Yes, my dear! You look ideal!
All the limelight you will steal!
Royal hearts will flutter faster.
For the plain, 't will be disaster.
Off you go! But take good care:
By twelve o'clock you must leave there.

Cinders   Midnight?

The Godmother   Yes. By twelve o'clock.
After that, expect a shock.
Your riches go, if you are late,
And rags again will be your fate ...

(**Cinders**, *looking lovely, then leaves for the Ball.
She is followed by* **The Coachman** *and* **The Six Grooms.**
The Godmother *waves happily. Then,* **The Godmother**
says)

... To the Palace, next we go
To see my Cinders steal the show!

Scene Two

(*In the Palace.* **Footmen** *stand around.* **The King, The Queen** *and* **The Prince** *come in with* **Their Guests** *and talk to them.*)

The King (*To a* **Lady Guest**)
    Nice of you to come, My Dear.

The Lady Guest   Good of you to ask me, Sir.

The King (*To* **Another Guest**)
    Don't go hungry. Eat your fill!

The Second Guest   Oh, I will, Sir. Sure, I will!

The King (*To* **Amanda**)
    Let me see, now. You are . . . Who?

Amanda   Amanda, Sir . . .

    (*She points to* **Belinda** *and says*)

    . . . My sister, too.

The King   Pleased to meet you. Know my son?

Belinda   The Prince is known to everyone.

The Prince (*Turning away, and saying to* **Himself**, *but aloud*)
    Oh, how awful! What a bore!
    Who let those two through the door?

The Queen (*To* **The King**)
    He don't like them. Pity he's
    Going to be so hard to please.
    Better if we move about.
    That'll help him sort them out . . .

    (*She says to* **A Footman**)

    . . . Tell the band to start to play.

The King   We'll start dancing. That's the way! . . .

    (*He speaks to* **Everybody**)

    . . . Now, my friends, we'll dance in twos!

Men! Stand by the girl you choose!
Prince! Prepare to start the Ball!
Pick the fairest girl of all!

Amanda (*To* **Belinda**)
'The fairest girl'? Of course, that's me!

Belinda   It's me, he means. You watch. You'll see!

Amanda   You'd best hide your ugly face!
It's a joke! It's a disgrace!

Belinda   Ho! Ho! Sister! How you jest!

Amanda   Quiet, you! You're just a pest!

(**A Footman** *comes in from outside and goes to* **The King.**)

The Footman   There's a Princess at the gate.
She is sorry she is late.

The King   What's she like?

The Footman   Sir, she's a beauty.

The King   Let the Door Man do his duty.
Hurry! Bring the Lady in!
We are ready to begin.

(**The Footman** *hurries away*)

The Queen (*To* **The King**)
That's an extra mouth to feed.

The King (*To* **The Queen**)
Beauty, Dear, is what we need.

(**Cinders** *comes into the room. All talking stops.*
Everyone *gazes at her.*)

Cinders (*Kneeling to* **The King**)
I am late, Sir. Sorry, too.
Please don't take too hard a view.

The King   Princess! Please! We are so glad
That you could join us . . .

12

(*He looks at* **The Prince** *and says*)

. . . And our lad.

The Prince That's the girl I hoped to see.
Surely she's the one for me. . .

(*He speaks to* **Cinders**)

. . . Will you, by a happy chance,
Join me, Lady, in a dance?

(*Music is played, and all dance –* **Cinders** *always with*
The Prince. *There are solo turns, and* **All** *clap. Then*
Servants *bring food, on trays.*)

The Prince (*To* **Cinders**)
Princess! Stop, and let us eat.
Starters; soups; delicious meat;
All the goodies cooks can make –
Ices; trifle; tipsy cake;
And, to wash them down, some wine.

Cinders Thank you, Sir. That sounds just fine.

(**The Prince** *and* **Cinders** *start to eat.*)

Amanda (*To* **Belinda**)
Don't you hate to see that pair
Stuffing both their faces there?

Belinda You're jealous, Sister. Given
The chance, you'd be in Heaven.

Amanda Supping with a stick like that?
I'd rather eat with our old cat.

The King (*To* **His Guests**)
Eat up! Eat up! It does me good
To see young folk enjoy their food.

(*A clock strikes twelve.* **Cinders** *counts the chimes*)

Cinders (*After the twelfth stroke*)

13

Twelve o'clock! How time does fly!
TWELVE O'CLOCK? Then so must I!
'Back to rags!' she said. That's me.
Oh, how silly can one be?

(*She runs out, leaving on the floor one of her slippers.*)

Amanda   She runs away, that Princess fair!

Belinda   Look! She's left a slipper there!

Amanda   See! The Prince has got it! So!

The Prince (*Holding the slipper*)
After her! Don't let her go!

(**Everyone in the Room** *chases after* **Cinders.**)

14

Scene Three

(The Kitchen in the Castle, again. **Buttons** *comes in.)*

Buttons *(Speaking to* **Himself**, *but aloud)*
Mice! And lizards! Everywhere!
Down the cellar! Up the stair!
I've seen a rat, too – very fat.
Where's our pussy? Where's our cat? . . .

(Then, he calls)

. . . Cinders! Cinders! Where are you?
Don't be scared. It's Buttons, true!
Have you finished all your chores?
Swept the chimney? Scrubbed the floors?
Can't you hear old Buttons call?
They'll be home soon, from the Ball.
They'll be weary. They'll be sore.
Don't you vex them any more . . .

*(***Cinders** *limps into the Kitchen. She is dirty and in rags again. Buttons says to her)*

. . . Hello, Sweetie. Where've you been?
Off in Dreamland? With the Queen?

Cinders   I've had enough. I want to weep.
I'm so weary. Let me sleep!

Buttons   You'll be woken, never fear,
When your sisters get back here.
Hist! I hear their coach wheels now.
Keep your head down! Let them row!

*(***Amanda** *and* **Belinda** *come into the Kitchen.)*

Amanda   What an evening!

Belinda   What a Ball!

Amanda   What an ending to it all!

15

Belinda (*Calling*)   Poppa! Momma! Gone to bed?

Amanda   Are you living? Are you dead?

The Baron (*Wearing pyjamas and coming into the Kitchen*)
  No. We're still around, My Pet.

The Baron's Wife (*Also in night clothes, following him*)
  We're not going to sleep just yet.

The Baron   We must hear your story, first.
  Wondering is always worst.

The Baron's Wife   Did you have a splendid Ball?

The Baron   Tell us, quick, about it all.
  Who was there . . .

The Baron's Wife   . . . And what they wore.

The Baron   What they did . . .

The Baron's Wife   . . . And lots, lots more . . .

Amanda   Fairest girl of all the great
  Was a Princess . . .

Belinda   . . . She came late.
  At the Prince, she set her cap.

Amanda   He, poor man, fell in the trap.

Belinda   Then, at twelve, she ran away.

Amanda   Why she went, we cannot say.

Belinda   As she fled, she left a shoe.

Amanda   Such a tiny slipper, too.

Belinda   All cried 'Stop!' but she would go.

Amanda   Where she went to, we don't know.

  (*A trumpet sounds outside the Castle.*)

The Baron   Hist! I hear a trumpet bring
  Some new tidings from the King.

  (*Into the Kitchen walk **Three Footmen.***)

16

The First Footman   From the Palace we are sent . . .

The Second Footman   . . . To find out where a lady went.

The Third Footman   We are seeking some one sweet . . .

The First Footman   . . . Who has very little feet.

The Second Footman   The Prince will marry some one dear
Who lost this slipper . . .

(*He holds up the slipper and says*)

. . . Is she here?

Amanda   Wed the Prince? That handsome male?
Let me try!

Belinda   You'll surely fail!

(**Amanda's** *foot will not go into the shoe.*)

The Third Footman   All the ladies of the Court
Have tiny feet – or so they thought.

The First Footman   When they tried to wear this shoe
They were disappointed, too.

Belinda (*To* **Amanda**)
My turn, now that you have tried.
I will be the Prince's bride.

(**Belinda's** *foot will not go into the slipper.*)

Amanda.   Hah! You laughed a bit too quick!
You're as vain as you are thick!

Cinders   Please may Cinders try the shoe?

Belinda (*To* **Cinders**)   What has this to do with you?

Amanda   Your place is by our kitchen sink!

Belinda   The Prince has taste! He'd never think . . .

The Baron (*Interrupting*)   To be fair, we really ought to
Let her try the shoe, my daughter.

Cinders   I would like to try it. *Please.*

Amanda   If you must. But what a squeeze!

(**The First Footman** *puts the slipper on* **Cinders'** *foot*)

The Baron   Squeeze? What nonsense! It's a fit!
Her foot was specially made for it.

The Baron's Wife   This is rubbish! All a dream!
One of MY girls must be Queen!

(**The Prince** *walks into the Kitchen.*)

The Prince (*To The Footmen*)   Well, my Footmen? Any joy?

The Baron (*To* **The Prince**)   Cinders fits the shoe, my boy!
Like a flash, her foot went in . . .

(*From a pocket,* **Cinders** *takes the other slipper and*
The Baron *says*)

. . . And in her pocket, there's its twin!

The Prince (*To* **Cinders**)
Clever girl! Come, be my wife!
We will have a happy life!

Cinders (*To* **The Prince**)
Oh, yes, please. I fancy you.
But . . .

(*She turns to* **Amanda** *and* **Belinda** *and says*)

. . . Sisters, you'll be happy, too.
To our Palace you can come.
You can use it as your home.
And we'll find you, each, a mate
From among the good and great . . .

(*She turns to* **Buttons** *and says*)

. . . Loving Buttons, I intend
To reward you, faithful friend.
Though my debt is, I would say,

More than Cinders can repay.

(**The Godmother** *comes into the Kitchen.*)

The Godmother   Cinders, for so long put down
Will now be giv'n a royal crown . . .

(*She says to* **The Audience**)

. . . For her wedding, she must dress,
So, excuse her, will you? Yes? . . .

(**Cinders** *leaves the Kitchen, to claps from* **All.** *Then* **The Godmother** *says to* **The Audience**)

. . . To the Palace, you're invited.
I'll be there. I feel excited.

Scene Four

(In the Palace again. **The King** *and* **Queen** *are greeting* **All Those They Have Invited to the Wedding.** **The Prince** *and* **Cinders** *are not yet to be seen.)*

The King Welcome one and welcome all.
Welcome short and welcome tall.
Welcome stout and welcome slender.
Welcome tough and welcome tender.
Welcome dark and welcome fair.
Welcome those with lots of hair.
Welcome old men, nearly bald.
Come, whatever name you're called.
Welcome! Welcome, everyone!
Walk right in and join the fun.
We're all set to have a fling.
Come and play and dance and sing.

The Queen Soon we'll see, with love and pride,
Our son, with Cinders by his side.

(Music is played while **Everyone Present** *waits patiently for the* **Royal Pair.***)*

The King *(Stopping the music)*
Here they come, the happy dears!
Let's all give them THREE LOUD CHEERS!

(And **The Prince** *and* **Cinders** *enter the room. Then, a big rejoicing can begin.)*

PRODUCTION NOTES

(For the children to use)

Stage directions

In the theatre, actors label the stage **left** and **right** as they face the audience. Then they use the words **stage right** and **stage left** to make rehearsal instructions very clear. They also say that they move **downstage** when they move towards the audience and **upstage** when they move away from the audience. You may like to use these words when you are rehearsing.

Settings

For this play, you will need to show two different settings – the Kitchen in the Baron's Castle, and the Ballroom in the Palace. There is no need to have a lot of complicated scenery. You can suggest the two settings by hanging at the back of the acting areas large wall paintings that suit each place. Another way: you can use changes in the colour of the stage lighting, if you have any. The two different atmospheres will be shown, too, by the costumes.

Here is one possible way of arranging the acting areas. (There are other ways, of course):

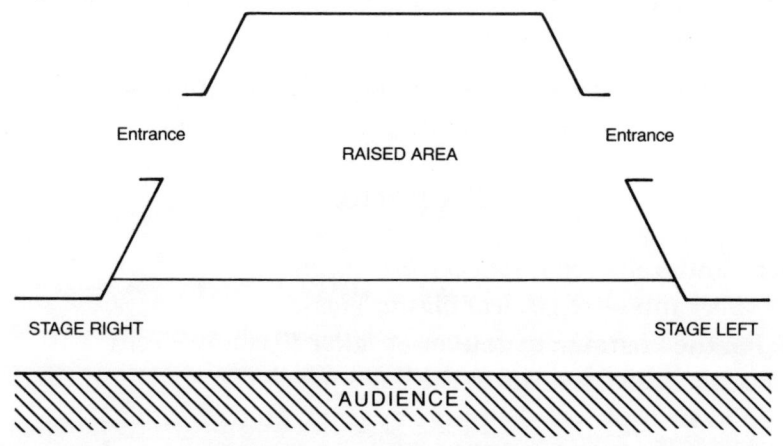

Costumes

You can have great fun designing your own costumes for this play. Here are some ideas that may help you with the more difficult costumes:

How to change rags to riches
Rags
1   Pink or white leotard underneath.
2   Make a grey, brown or dirty-coloured skirt to wrap around the waist.
3   Use a dirty-looking shawl to tie around the shoulders.
Riches
1   Remove dirty skirt and shawl.
2   Add skirt, pale in colour.
3   Wear jewellery.

How to change a day dress into a ball gown
1   Begin with a roll of material tied round the waist, to make very wide hips.
2   Add a long skirt of bright colours to a contrasting T-shirt. Now you have a *day dress*.
3   Add a wrapover skirt in another bright colour, to make a *ball gown* which decorates the day dress under it.

Wedding dress
Add overskirt of white and a veil.

Materials to use: old nightdresses; crêpe paper; ribbons; etc.
Buttons can wear a jacket with buttons sewn all over it.

Properties

Collect: Cinderella – *mop, bucket, broom, etc.*
          Servants – *trays; clear plastic 'glasses'.*
Make: For the Postman to deliver – *a letter* 30 cm by 15 cm.
          For all Ladies who go to the Ball – *jewels* (Thread 'junk' material on to string or wool. Spray or paint it gold or silver.)

mirrors (Cut the shapes you want from stiff card. Then fix some silver paper on to them with glue.)
Fans (Fold thin card. Decorate it with felt tip pens or paint.)
a box of wigs

How to make a wig
1   Blow up a round balloon and fasten it.
2   Tie a piece of string to it and hang it up.
3   Cover it with 3 or 4 layers of torn paper and cold-water paste.
4   Allow the paper to dry hard.
5   Burst the balloon, leaving a hollow shape of hard paper.
6   Cut it so that it will show your face and allow you to put it on your head comfortably.
7   Make hair by gluing wool, string, curled paper or wood shavings – or anything else you think would look effective – on to the mould you have made.
8   Spray on bright colours or decorate with ribbons.

For the Guests at the Ball, food can be made with papier mâché. This, when dry, can be painted.

Sound effects

You can try to compose your own music, using percussion instruments, guitars, recorders, etc. There may be someone in your company who can play a piano. You will need music for the start and the ending of the play, as well as for the Ball in the Palace.

For the clock chimes you can use a triangle, or notes on a xylophone or glockenspiel.

For the trumpet, you can use a real instrument, if you have a brass player in your company. If you haven't, you can imitate the sound of a trumpet with your voices, using the words 'PAH! PAH! PAH!' BBC Sound Effects records are often helpful.

TEACHER'S NOTES

Improvisation

This play requires the children to play 'larger-than-life' characters. The following ideas for improvisation are intended to give the preliminary experience needed for the actors and actresses to play the parts with conviction.

All drama lessons should have a structure starting with a warm-up, developing into a main activity, and ending with a wind-down. Depending on the space and time available and the ability of the children, a selection can be made from the following:

Starters
Play some lively music. Let the children dance freely to it for a few moments. Then ask them to work out their own sequences of movements to a section of the music. They can then choose partners, and work in pairs. The number in each group can be increased at the teacher's discretion.

Development
Sound Mirrors   The children work in pairs. One speaks very slowly, leading the way. The other tries to copy, 'mirroring' whatever the first is saying. Soon, the first should start to exaggerate – speaking faster and more loudly; making more dramatic gestures; and so on.
Bullies   In pairs, the children construct an argument using these sentences only: 'I want it', 'You've got it' and 'I'm going to take it!'
Whatever I do is wrong   The children work in threes. A gives an order. B carries it out. C criticises B, however well he/she has fulfilled A's instructions. Then roles are exchanged.
Success against all odds   In small groups the children can discuss this title. Then they can play out a scene that illustrates it.

Wind-down
The children stand separately. Then they should feel and think in a smaller and smaller way, as though they are shrinking. As they do so, they get closer to the ground, and gradually they become part of it. Then they relax; count ten; and finish.

Follow-up Work

Whether the children read, perform or watch this play, the teacher may like to develop their participation with these suggestions:

Reading
Cinderella was originally written down by Charles Perrault (1628–1703). Other famous tales recorded by him were *Bluebeard, Red Riding Hood* and *Sleeping Beauty*.

Writing
Write a story entitled *Cinder Fella*. What would have happened if the principal character had been a boy who had 'Ugly Step Brothers'? Would events have been different from those in *Cinderella?*

Art and Craft
Make a cartoon strip of the story of *Cinderella*.
With clay, plasticine or papier mâché, make models of the animals in the story.
Make decorative fans.
Decorate an old shoe so that it becomes a 'magic slipper'.
Design some special make-up for the Ugly Sisters.

First published 1987

Published by
MACMILLAN EDUCATION LTD
Houndmills, Basingstoke, Hampshire RG21 2XS
and London
Companies and representatives
throughout the world

Additional material
written by Ginny Lapage

Typeset by Regent Typesetting

Printed in Hong Kong

Cover: Margaret Sherry

Williams, Guy R.
Cinderella.—(Junior dramascripts)
I. Title   II. Lapage, Ginny   III. Series
822'.914   PR6073,1426/

ISBN 0-333-43382-3